Build A Better Board In 30 Days

This Book is a Gift

From:

_____

To:

_____

by

Carol Weisman

Published by:
F.E. Robbins & Sons Press
St. Louis, Missouri
October, 1998

Second Printing – September, 1999

Bulk purchase rates available

Copyright © 1998 by Board Builders
48 Granada Way
St. Louis MO 63124
1-888-500-1777
FAX 314-991-3018
E-mail CEWFER@aol.com

Cover by Ad Graphics, Tulsa OK 918 252-1103
Photo by VIP Graphics

Printed in the United States of America.

ISBN 0-9666168-0-4

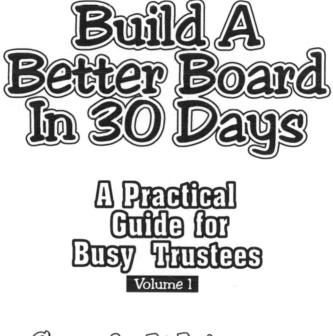

Build A Better Board In 30 Days

A Practical Guide for Busy Trustees

Volume 1

Carol Weisman

Dedication

To Steve Epner, my friend and
mentor, who always has a new
toy or magic trick, a joke and
an encouraging word.

Preface

Years ago, a generous board member gave all of us on a board copies of "The Board Member's Book," by Brian O'Connell. It is a marvelous book, but rather daunting. It took me 10 years to actually get around to reading it.

In contrast, this is a little book to help conscientious board members and staff do a better job. All you need is a long coffee break or a short plane flight to get through the whole thing.

Having served on 21 boards and been president of seven as well as having worked with countless boards, I've learned from the best and the worst. My hope is that you can share in the joys and avoid the potholes.

Few boards will be able to implement all of the ideas in this book. Depending on the size, age, staffing, funding needs and mission of your organization, some ideas will make more sense than others.

There is no particular order as to when to do things. Implement what makes sense for you today.

My hope is that there will be a few ideas that will make your board service more productive and rewarding for both you and those you serve.

Acknowledgments

Special thanks to my literary friends, poet Mary Ann Blank and happily retired Tillingite Pat Webb, for slogging through all of my dyslexic mistakes and making corrections. Babette Morgan, you are a fabulous editor and friend. Jim Weems at Ad Graphics, how are you always so helpful and cheerful?

Thanks to Linda Nash for urging me to finish this book.

I want to thank VIP Graphics for their help with my cover photo. (My image of myself is Sharon Stone with underwear and a sense of humor-even though I actually look more like John Goodman.) You did the very best you could.

Caty Griesedieck, thanks for painting

my hard hat. You are always there for me!

I breathe easy knowing that friend and perfectionist Karen Pic will be managing distribution.

But most of all, I want to thank the colleagues, friends, clients and fellow board members who gave me all of these great ideas. Folks like Carolyn McDole, Dale Mintz, Mark Rubin, Sy Friedland, Reed Dewey, Steve Bajardi, Kathleen King, Celeste Prussia, Barbara Boyle, Barbara Bennett, Sheryl Silvey, Mark LeBlanc, Christain Arden-Joley and Sharon Rohrbach. You make my work a joy.

And, as always, special thanks to my sister Dr. Nancy Wilking (if you need a Gyn in Baltimore, call her) and to the three men I love, Frank, Teddy and Jono Robbins.

Day
1

Become
a fly
on the wall

BOARD BUILDERS

Notes:

What is it like to be a customer of your nonprofit? Are the staff members polite and helpful? Are the facilities clean? How are the phones answered? Are they answered? Do you wind up in voice-mail hell? Take a serious look around.

Speak to clients as well. If your agency is in the performing arts, chat with the audience at intermission; if you are a food pantry, sit in the waiting area for a morning and observe.

Even very dingy places can feel like a warm hug when people are treated with kindness and respect.

If you find things that could be improved upon, speak with the CEO and ask, "What can I do to make it better?"

For example: "Can I ask a friend who

13

has an interior design studio about getting some window treatments donated? Can I ask my son's Boy Scout troop if it would be willing to paint? Does our staff need some customer-service training? How can I get them support?"

Even more important, ask yourself, "What is right about our place? What makes people want to come? What should we preserve?"

Day
2

Ask how you can work better with the staff

Notes:

ood relationships between board members and paid staff can be tricky. One group does its work during "normal" working hours and the other group in its spare time. Discussing when and how it is most efficient to communicate will avert a lot of misunderstandings. For instance, you may welcome a call at 6 in the morning, but not at 6 at night. A staff member may never want to be called on a Saturday unless it's an emergency.

With e-mail, voice mail, answering machines and faxes, there are many ways to transmit information other than the traditional face-to-face meeting. Discuss which method is best for you and for the staff member with whom you work.

Discuss the amount of detail you

want on various issues so that you will feel informed but not overwhelmed.

Also agree on a "no secrets policy" so that if a major problem arises, a commitment is made to notify you immediately.

Finally, ask, "What can I do to make your job easier?" And mean it then do it! (Feel free to try this at home as well!)

Take a funder to lunch... don't ask for money

BOARD BUILDERS

Notes:

Imagine people always being interested in what they can get from you and never being interested in you. That's why it's important to stay in touch with individual donors or corporate giving officers without always bringing up what they can do for your agency. Get to know the people behind the checkbooks.

If you don't have the best memory, keep notes. When you meet again, you'll remember to ask about the new baby or the trip to take a son to college.

Stay in touch in good times and bad. If a company is experiencing scandal or fiscal problems, send a note to your contact. Express nonjudgmental concern. If you expect these folks to care about your cause, you also need to care about them.

When one company with a history of giving went into chapter 11, a nonprofit board sent a 5-pound box of nuts with a note that read "Nuts to your creditors, we still love you." When the company came out of Chapter 11, guess who it sent its first check to? Had it gone under, its employees would have gone to other companies where they might have been able to help.

Kindness pays. You feel good, they feel good, and you are able to fund your mission.

Day
4

Thank a
secretary

BOARD BUILDERS

Notes:

Executives don't run the world. Secretaries do. Secretaries are the gatekeepers to power. Put the first and last name of your board members' secretaries on your board roster.

When a secretary or administrative assistant or spouse has been particularly helpful, send a note, a card, or a gift. If a whole group proved helpful, call and ask if you can bring lunch for the gang.

A case in point: Once, a secretary helped on a fund raiser by tracking her boss from Brazil to Cambodia to verify a prize for a nonprofit auction.

The prize was valued at more than $10,000, so the auction chair wanted to make sure it appeared accurately in the program book. Two free tickets for the auction, a plant and a thank-you note helped make the secretary both a friend and donor.

When talking with secretaries, ask if they are interested in volunteering. These are people who are already willing to help.

Be sure to add secretaries to your mailing lists to receive newletters and requests for funds.

Day
5

Design a quiz for your board and staff

BOARD BUILDERS

Notes:

You can't sell a product you don't know. One of the duties of the board is to sell the mission of its nonprofit to community leaders and funders.

Design a quiz for your fellow board members that includes questions about your history, bylaws and the services you deliver. If you are a shelter for battered women, ask how many children were housed how many nights. How many women and children were turned away because there was no room?

If you are an arts organization, your board and staff should know how many folks listened to, viewed or visited your venue.

Be sure to include financial data about your organization. Many computer software programs can help you turn questions into word puzzles.

Give your board "the elevator test." This is where you have to be able to explain your mission in the time it would take to get from the fifth floor to the ground floor.

Have prizes. Have fun. Get smart.

Find your
successor

BOARD BUILDERS

Notes:

You've joined the board of a non-profit organization, not the bench of the United States Supreme Court. This is not a lifetime appointment.

Looking for a replacement early provides an escape route should you be unable to fulfill your duties for any reason and empowers other board members by succession planning.

When searching for a replacement do not promise that your choice will have your position when you vacate it. You may not have that authority, and if the person does a poor job, you will want the option to look elsewhere.

To groom a likely candidate, ask him or her to co-chair a committee or project with you. This is an opportunity to impart knowledge and to find out how the other person works.

Your successor should have an understanding of the mission of your organization, an ability to adapt to or improve the culture of the organization, and finally, an ability to motivate and work with people.

Finding a replacement will ensure the future of your nonprofit and promote your own mental health.

Day
7

Thank a merchant

BOARD BUILDERS

Notes:

Folks in retail are always getting hit up for items for special events or for direct use by clients.

The next time you are in one of their businesses, thank them at the point of sale. It doesn't matter if the person you thank isn't the decision-maker. Thank the waitress or the clerk or the manager. Let each of them know that the philanthropic behavior of their employer is appreciated in the community. Describe what a difference their company makes.

Take names if the people you thank show interest. Get them involved in your next event.

Bring their business cards to your next board meeting and pass them out.

Call a board member who's missed a meeting

BOARD BUILDERS

Notes:

A nyone who's missed a meeting should be called by either another board member or by a staff person. The first question should always be "How are you?" Then stop and listen.

Sometimes meetings are missed because a board member just lost a parent, is ill, is involved in a corporate takeover, or is still fuming over the last meeting.

Whatever the reason, find out and take appropriate action. If the reason is personal, ask if you may share it with the board. For instance, consider the board member who was too ashamed to show up because he had just lost his job. He assumed the board was only interested in him because of his corporate connection.

With permission from the member, the board chair sent out a fax with "the good news" that Ken was for hire. Ken had another job within a month.

If an absence is going to be prolonged, perhaps because of a major illness, make plans for another member to complete any work the sick person was busy with.

If a board member was just too busy, fill her in on the meeting and tell her you look forward to seeing her at the next one.

Care about your board members, and they'll care about you.

Mail the agenda at least a week before the meeting

BOARD BUILDERS

Notes:

Most board members enjoy doing a good job and prefer not
to look foolish in public. Asking for a report at a board meeting from
a board member who is unprepared is
no way to promote good trusteeship.

Look for easier, cheaper and quicker
ways than the U.S. Postal Services to
disseminate the agenda. Some groups
use e-mail or fax broadcast. If there are
attachments, those can also be sent in
advance.

Use fax-on-demand when board
members want additional detail if it's
available, such as more detailed financial information. The object is to get
everyone to the meeting ready to make
informed decisions.

Offer more detailed information, for

example, a copy of the audit to all who want it well in advance of the meeting.

The board is the organization's ambassador to the community. Help them be as informed as possible.

Day
10

Organize a thankathon

BOARD BUILDERS

Notes:

Asking for money is hard for most people. Thanking people tends to be far more comfortable.

Rather than organizing a phonathon to ask for money, ask a board member to organize a thankathon. It works the same except that you are thanking people for having given.

A script might read: "This is Mary Smith of The National Kidney Foundation. This is not a call to ask for anything. I just want to thank you for the generous donation of your car. Thanks to people like you..." and tell what you have been able to do because of their generosity.

Then you listen. During this conversation, you may find a potential volunteer, client, board member or major donor. Or you may have a chance to say only a quick thank-you.

Make sure you have a written record of the call for follow-up purposes.

This is not an alternative to a written thank-you letter. It is a way to reach out, board member to donor, and a first step in getting your board involved in the development process.

Day 11

Make name tents

Notes:

P eople do better in meetings when they know one another's names. Unless you've had the same board for years (in which case you need to reconvene the nominating committee), you need a way to identify one another.

The advantage of a name tent versus a name tag is size. You can read a name tent from across a room. You can make a name tent by printing on card stock with 90-point type and then folding the paper in half so that it will stand up on the table.

The great question then becomes how to creatively use the side facing the board member.

Too often, we're in meetings discussing trivia and thinking about being at the sale at the mall or on the golf course.

The other side of the name tent can help us focus. One idea is to put the mission statement on the side facing the board member. Another is to put a graphic representation of the mission. For instance, an environmental group might put a picture of a toxic waste dump, an arts group, an empty stage. Find a creative board member to take on this project.

Ask a corporation for something other than money

BOARD BUILDERS

Notes:

orporations have great "stuff" other than money. Too often we go in and think only of getting a financial contribution.

First and foremost, corporations have people. If you need an army for a specific project, ask a corporation new to your nonprofit to recruit its employees. Remember, 80 percent of all donations are made by individuals, so get the home address of each volunteer for a personal thank-you and an opportunity to ask each to help out later.

If you ask for support on a special project, be prepared to tell the management of the company how you will help promote their product. Whether it is the company name on a program or a building, you need to acknowledge help in a manner the donor finds acceptable.

Corporations also employ folks with specific skills. You may want to ask a corporation for 20 hours of its advertising or auditing department's time.

Keep a lookout for new board members. A friend on the inside is always welcome.

Ask who knows your potential funders

BOARD BUILDERS

Notes:

One of the major duties of your board is to ensure the financial viability of your organization.

When you are approaching individuals, corporations or foundations, look within the board for help.

A list of pending grants should be a part of the board minutes or sent out regularly by fax broadcast or e-mail. If a board member has an "in," a letter of support should be included with grant applications. Sometime an "in" is based on friendship, sometimes a business relationship. For instance, if you are applying to a bank for funding and one of your board members owns a corporation that does business there, a letter of support will obviously have value.

Also, find out the names of the decision-makers, and circulate them among your board members. Sometimes a five-minute call from a board member who is a friend of the decision-maker can make all the difference.

Day
14

Plan a board retreat

BOARD BUILDERS

Notes:

Board members need time to share vision, to deepen their understanding of their organization's mission, and to gel as a team. Board retreats are the ideal time to relax away from the clock and look at the bigger issues.

A board retreat can be a half-day on a weekend in town or two days away from where the board normally meets.

The biggest challenge is getting people to commit the time. A retreat should be announced at least six months in advance to get it onto everyone's calendars.

Your best special-events person should be in charge of the structure of the meeting to make sure it contains a component of fun.

Some boards find it helpful at a retreat to bring in an outside consultant to help plow through what can be difficult or contentious issues.

Always include team-building activities. One of my favorites is to divide the board into groups of three and to ask members of each group to find three things they have in common. Then share with the whole group to see if others also have these in common.

Read the newspaper with an eye toward recruiting

BOARD BUILDERS

Notes:

Who are the top volunteer leaders in your community and why? Whose names always appear in the newspaper. Start tracking these folks. Call one and ask him or her to lunch. If she is too busy to meet right now, ask if you could take a minute of her time to tell her about your organization. Ask when her term as president of the group she now chairs is up. Can you send her material? Invite her as your guest to your next function.

Top leaders may have commitments to other organizations for two or three years, but many of these people are worth waiting for. As much as people talk about looking forward to being a "past president" rather than a president of an organization, there is a real sense of loss for many when their terms end.

This is the time to get a superstar involved with your group.

Superstars are the board members who come with a four-star Rolodex, who know the press, and write checks. They take time to cultivate. Begin now for the board of the future.

Take a look at your 990 form

BOARD BUILDERS

Notes:

The 990 is the form every nonprofit with a budget of $25,000 or more has to file with the Internal Revenue Service. This document is open to the public.

It is the obligation of nonprofits to make the annual returns for the past three years available to the public. However, your group does not have to disclose the names of donors.

Information on the 990 includes the salaries of the top five employees as well as the names of the officers of the board of directors. The president has to sign the form as well as the executive director.

The 990 form is frequently requested by funders. Take a good look at the form with this thought in mind.

Be sure you know the information included in your 990 when you make a solicitation call.

The IRS has a great websitewith a list of Frequently Asked Questions. The site is:

www.irs.ustreas.gov/prod/bus_info/ eo-faqs.html

Ask the nominating committee to design a letter of commitment

BOARD BUILDERS

Notes:

A void the "moi" syndrome. This is where a board member is asked to do something, for instance raise money, and with a startled look, he or she declares "moi!"

Board members need to know what it means to be a good board member. Every year the nominating committee needs to draw up a letter of commitment that includes the following information: term of office, times and dates of meetings, committee assignments, financial and attendance guidelines, as well as other expectations, such as, "Bring at least two foursomes to the fund-raising golf tournament."

When a board member joins, he or she is then asked to sign on the dotted line, send in a copy and keep a copy.

It's good to find out early that your

marvelous recruit can't make any meetings on Tuesdays, which is your standard board meeting day.

The clearer you are, the greater your chances of having an efficient and enthusiastic board.

This is also a marvelous exercise for current board members to assess their service.

Day
18

Make friends
with two
Realtors®

Notes:

R ealtors are like barbers, bartenders and psychiatrists. They know about the wants and needs of people.

You need to have two friends who are real estate agents: one residential and one commercial.

When people move, one of the things they miss most are the friendships, as well as the connectedness, they found through their volunteer work.

Find an agent who is working with high-end properties and ask to be included in lunch meetings with people who may have the time and interest to get involved in nonprofit groups like yours.

A commercial agent will know of new businesses coming into town, as well as people who may have a few thousand square feet of space they aren't using. And if there is a new company coming to town, shouldn't its grand opening be a benefit for your group?

What about some free office space, even if it is only for six months or a year to house a short-term project?

Commercial real estate agents also know who is moving away and what equipment they may want to donate.

Day
19

Write a
check

BOARD BUILDERS

Notes:

One hundred percent giving is the name of the game. It is the responsibility of board leadership to write the first checks for any board-initiated program in which the community is asked to donate.

If you as board members don't care enough to give, why should the community? Being able to say to a potential funder "Our board has supported this project 100 percent" is a powerful position.

Who should ask board members to give? Other board members. This should not be a staff function. At the end of the year, a letter of thanks (preferably not a form letter) should go out to each board member. It should be something like this:

Dear Harvey,

What would we have done if you hadn't chaired the golf tournament. As always, you did a marvelous job. Thanks to you and your committee, we will be able to increase services by 12 percent this year, which means 75 more children will be able to....

As you well know, in addition to work, we need good old money. I hope you will be as generous with your checkbook as you have been with your time. It's an honor to serve with you.

Sincerely,

the Board Chair.

Day
20

Look for a
friend
in the food
industry

Notes:

Whether feeding ballet dancers, children with cancer or serving an alumni luncheon, nonprofits travel on their bellies. Having a friend in the food industry can drastically cut your bottom line. Whether it's a connection with the fanciest four-star restaurant, a fast-food chain, grocery store or beverage company, these folks can mobilize armies to help you either serve your clients directly or raise funds.

Don't overlook large organizations in this field, such as a restaurant association or the dairy council .

Look to colleges and universities for food-preparation or hotel and restaurant management programs; they may have students interested in volunteering.

Some nonprofits are getting into the catering business themselves and using the business to help train clients for jobs in the food service industry while providing low-cost food for groups.

Shop the competition

Notes:

J ust as Wal-Mart knows what Kmart is up to, and Saks keeps an eye on Neiman Marcus, your nonprofit should be watching its competition.

Ask to be on the mailing list for a competitor's newsletter. Send in a contribution and see how the group responds. Go to one of its fund-raisers. How are people being treated? Are volunteers in attendance? What about the board?

You can also get a copy of any group's 990, the federal income tax form filed by all nonprofits with a budget greater than $25,000. With information from these forms, you can get an idea whether you are paying your staff well enough to be competitive.

Look to nonprofits in other fields to

see what they are doing. If you are a disease-focused group, look to the arts, and vice versa. What do you learn by reading their annual reports about how you can do business better?

Day
22

Honor a
board member

BOARD BUILDERS

Notes:

There are great debates as to why people give of their time and many right answers. Some stand by the idea that people who serve shouldn't need to be recognized. But people are, in fact, motivated by recognition.

Make plans for an ABCD (above and beyond the call of duty) Award or other award for that one board member who always goes the distance. Then make plans to give the award where it will have the most meaning for the member.

Imagine the surprise when the board president and executive director pop out of a closet at a board member's staff meeting to honor an executive who has given not only of himself, but involved his whole company.

And picture the delight of another board member when she is surprised not just by an award at a board meeting but also by the presence of her husband, who flew in her folks and brought her sister and the kids along too.

Maybe just doing good should be enough, but folks thrive on recognition, and it inspires others.

Be there for your corporate friends

BOARD BUILDERS

Notes:

If a friend has surgery, you send flowers. If a friend has a triumph, you celebrate. The same should be true of your corporate friends.

For instance, during a merger or downsizing, send a kind note saying "Thinking of you at XYZ Corporation. This can't be easy." It takes five minutes and means so much.

If your organization offers a specific service that may be of value to a corporation in trouble, offer to help. This is especially true of social service agencies, but arts agencies can also help by offering tickets or a special performance.

If your corporate friend has just won a big contract, send a big banner signed with well-wishes from the board and staff of your organization.

Remember, corporations are made up of people. Ask yourself what you would do if your best friend were going through what your corporate supporter is experiencing, and act accordingly.

Write a press release about each of your board members

BOARD BUILDERS

Notes:

N onprofit groups rarely have enormous marketing budgets. Yet we all need to get the news about our nonprofit out to as many folks as possible. We also need to promote and thank our board members for their dedicated service.

Send press releases with each board member's permission to each of their colleges, universities, grad schools, high schools, churches and employers, mentioning the work they have done on your behalf. Suggest to each of these schools that they write a story featuring the involvement of their graduate in your organization. Some universities send out as many as 200,000 copies of their alumni publications. Some corporations have similar circulations of internal and external publications.

Ask a board member with an interest in public relations to write up the press releases. Make sure you get permission from your board member.

Write a
detailed
board list

BOARD BUILDERS

Notes:

Most board lists contain the name of the board member, address, phone number, plus a fax number and e-mail address. I would like to suggest including a lot more information. You just never know when you can use it. Include:

- Secretary's first and last name.

- Board member's birthday (year optional).

- Spouse's first and last name.

- Spouse's employment information.

- Names, ages and schools or occupations of children.

- Board member's high school, college, and graduate school.

- Other volunteer involvement.

- Other board affiliations (include for-profit boards).
- Club memberships.
- Preferred means of communication, i.e., e-mail versus fax or phone.
- Special dietary needs
- Transportation preferences i.e. specific airline, seat location or handicapped van
- Home phone number for emergencies
- Beeper number
- Car phone number

Day
26

Cruise the nonprofit sites on the net

Notes:

The Internet provides some wonderful electronic newsletters of interest to those of us involved with nonprofits. Some of my favorites are as follows:

The National Center For Nonprofit Boards: wwwncnb.org/home.html

Society for Nonprofit Organizations: www.danenet.wicip.org/snpo

Nonprofit Times: www.nptimes.com/

Aspen Institute: Nonprofit Sector Research Fund: www.aspeninst. org/dir/polpro/NSRF/NSRF1.html

Energize: www.energizeinc.com

Foundation Center fdncenter.org/grantmaker/contents.html

Philanthropy News Digest fdncenter.org/phil/philmain.html

Nonprofit Resources Catalogue: www.clar4k.net80/pub/pwalker/ home.html

Carnegie Library Foundation Center: alphaclp.clpgh.org/CLP/Foundation/ fchome.html

National Society of Fund Raising Executives: www.nsfre.org/

Subscribe to a nonprofit journal

BOARD BUILDERS

Notes:

There are several great resources that deliver the latest information on philanthropy and governance. Here are two:

The National Center for Nonprofit Boards in Washington, D.C., produces many marvelous books and pamphlets on all aspects of governance. It also holds a national leadership conference every year in November in Washington, D.C., featuring the best and the brightest authorities on governance from around the world. You can call them at 1-800-883-6262 for more information, or visit their web site at www.ncnb.org/home.html

My other favorite resource for nonprofit news is "Nonprofit World" published by the Society for Nonprofit Organizations, Madison, Wisconsin. This is a journal with articles covering everything from new legislation for directors and officers to insurance, nonprofit mergers, and the latest in fund-raising techniques. You can subscribe by calling 1-800-424-7367. Their web site is http://danenet.wicip.org/snpo

Tell them Carol sent ya!

Day
28

Send your staff for training

BOARD BUILDERS

Notes:

How would you feel if your doctor, your lawyer or your dentist did not pursue continuing education? We all want state-of-the-art care.

How do you feel when you come home from a conference? Most of us come home invigorated, renewed and ready to face new challenges.

As the nonprofit sector becomes more sophisticated and complex, our nonprofit managers need to keep up. Yet many small nonprofits do not budget funds for professional development for staff. Allocating money for continuing education is a solid move toward ensuring the future of your agency and toward retaining the loyalty and commitment of an increasingly knowledgeable staff.

If you don't have a lot of time or money, check out the latest programs available thru distance education provided by:

The Learning Institute
for Nonprofit Organizations
800-214-8326

E-mail:
LINST@danenet.wicip.org

web site:
www.uwex.edu/li/

The National Center
for Nonprofit Boards
800-883-6262

web site:
www.ncnb.org/home.html

Read your bylaws

BOARD BUILDERS

Notes:

Bylaws are the skeleton of an organization. They are the bones that hold up the entire structure.

Unfortunately, there are two types of bylaws: fiction and nonfiction. Bylaws become fiction when members don't know what they contain.

What are the terms of office? What constitutes a quorum?

Remember, as a board member of a nonprofit, you are both legally and morally responsible for ensuring that the mission is carried out.

As part of orientation, make sure members read the bylaws. One of the duties of the board secretary is to make sure bylaws are available during meetings.

Every few years, a committee needs

to review the bylaws to make sure the nonprofit is in compliance and to make suggestions for changes where necessary.

Bring a speaker to your board meeting

BOARD BUILDERS

Notes:

The most memorable board meetings happen when something out of the ordinary occurs. Bring in a provocative speaker on an issue related to your mission. For instance, if you are a drug-treatment facility, invite the local coroner or prosecuting attorney. If you are an arts group, bring in a curator or private collector. Just make sure your guest is a good speaker with something to say.

If the material is difficult to process, you may want to schedule the meeting in the evening so that your board members don't have to go on to work after a highly emotional session.

An occasional evening meeting also presents an opportunity for board members to socialize and bond.

Day
31

Underpromise
and
overdeliver

Notes:

There are two schools of thought on goal-setting. One is to set an unattainable goal and work like mad to get there. I prefer to set an attainable goal and overdo it.

For instance, I think a goal of 100 percent giving for a board is great and attainable. But what do you think a funder would say if you went in and said, "Not only does our board give at the 100 percent level, but 40 percent of the companies our board members work for also give either money or resources, and of our board members who have secretaries, 60 percent are also donors. Not only that, but for the evening party before our board retreat, 80 percent of the spouses and significant others show up. And, furthermore, 45 percent of our board members have our nonprofit in their wills."

Set what you consider a minimum goal, and then work like mad to exceed it in every possible way.

About the Author

Carol Weisman has served on 21 boards and been president of seven. She started her professional career as a social worker working with street gangs, the perfect background for working with boards. She found many of the gangs better organized and with more successful fund-raising programs (which she clearly doesn't recommend).

She then worked for many years as a medical social worker at St. Louis Children's Hospital and Children's Hospital National Medical Center.

Carol lives with Frank Robbins, her sweet, long-suffering husband of 23 years. They have two sons in college, Teddy (also known as Frank) at New

York University and Jono at Alfred University.

When not traveling the world keynoting, facilitating and training, Carol serves on the board of Women's Self Help Center, is president of the Gateway Chapter of the National Speakers Association and volunteers for the Learning Disabilities Association.

Thank you for buying this book. The boys' tuition is due, and Carol is over her Mastercard limit!